Castles & Cottages

RIVER RETREATS OF THE THOUSAND ISLANDS

THIS BOOK IS DEDICATED TO SUE HALSEY AND TED MOWERS.
WHENEVER TED AND I WERE TOGETHER ON HIS BOAT ON
THE ST. LAWRENCE RIVER WE MANAGED TO SHAKE UP THE WORLD.
GF

Castles & Cottages

RIVER RETREATS OF THE THOUSAND ISLANDS

PHOTOGRAPHY BY GEORGE FISCHER

TEXT BY ANTHONY MOLLICA JR.

The BOSTON
MILLS PRESS

www.bostonmillspress.com

A BOSTON MILLS PRESS BOOK

Copyright © 2004 George Fischer

Second Printing, 2005

National Library of Canada Cataloguing in Publication

Fischer, George, 1954-
Castles and cottages : river retreats of the Thousand Islands / photographs by George Fischer ; text by Anthony Mollica, Jr.

Includes bibliographical references.
ISBN 1-55046-398-5

1. Historic buildings—Thousand Islands (N.Y. and Ont.)—Pictorial works. 2. Dwellings—Thousand Islands (N.Y. and Ont.)—Pictorial works.
3. Historic buildings—Thousand Islands (N.Y. and Ont.). 4. Dwellings—Thousand Islands (N.Y. and Ont.) 5. Thousand Islands
(N.Y. and Ont.)—Biography. 6. Thousand Islands (N.Y. and Ont.)—History. I. Mollica, Anthony, 1939- II. Title.

FC3095.T43F58 2004   971.3'7   C2003-907090-5

Publisher Cataloging-in-Publication Data (U.S.)

Fischer, George.
Castles and cottages : river retreats of the Thousand Islands / photographs by George Fischer ; text by Anthony Mollica.—1st ed..
[96] p. : col. photos. ; cm.
Includes bibliographical references.

Summary: A view of the buildings, builders and residents of the cottages and castles of the Thousand Islands of the St. Lawrence River:.
ISBN 1-55046-398-5

1. Architecture, Domestic— Thousand Islands (N.Y.and Ont.). 2. Thousand Islands (N.Y. and Ont.) — Homes and haunts — History.
3. Mansions — Thousand Islands (N.Y. and Ont.) — History. I. Mollica, Anthony. II. Title.

728.72/ 09713 dc22   NA7579.C2.F57   2004

PUBLISHED BY BOSTON MILLS PRESS
132 Main Street, Erin, Ontario, Canada N0B 1T0
Tel 519-833-2407 • Fax 519-833-2195 • e-mail: books@bostonmillspress.com • www.bostonmillspress.com

IN CANADA:
Distributed by Firefly Books Ltd.
66 Leek Crescent, Richmond Hill, Ontario, Canada L4B 1H1

IN THE UNITED STATES:
Distributed by Firefly Books (U.S.) Inc.
P.O. Box 1338, Ellicott Station, Buffalo, New York, USA 14205

Jacket: Gillian Stead   Book: McCorkindale Advertising & Design

Printed in Canada

The publisher acknowledges for the financial support of our publishing program
the Canada Council, the Ontario Arts Council, and the Government of Canada
through the Book Publishing Industry Development Program (BPIDP).

Contents

Foreword

The Thousand Islands—actually a group of nearly 1,800 islands—comprise a region that stretches about 50 miles downriver from the western head of the St. Lawrence River where it joins the eastern basin of Lake Ontario. These islands range in size from tiny outcroppings supporting a tree or two to large tracts of land containing small communities, farms and parks. The archipelago, mostly carved from Precambrian Shield granite by the St. Lawrence River, is a picturesque garden of woods and water that has lured tourists with its scenery for generations.

Scenic boat tours through the Thousand Islands have been offered since the late 1800s. Today, several boat lines based in the United States and Canada offer hundreds of thousands of tourists a glimpse of the region each year from their decks. Their popularity is clearly enhanced by the fact that the scenery is a rich blend of natural beauty and architectural charm.

The architecture of the Thousand Islands reflects a unique lifestyle. Life in the Thousand Islands is all about the river. Locals and seasonal residents alike refer to the St. Lawrence simply as "The River." The river is their retreat, recreation, entertainment, inspiration, and tradition.

It is only natural that a shoreline view is one of the most prized features of any home on the river. But a view of the river is not simply about the scenery. A proper view will draw the tension from your body at the end of a long week. It will inform you when the weather is right for fishing or boating. It will call from memory precious times spent with children, parents and friends. Views of the grand St. Lawrence can open the mind's creativity and offer peace in a chaotic world.

For generations, people have been building homes, cottages and even castles with a mind toward maximizing their connection with the river. In the mid-nineteenth century, summer homes were constructed by millionaires, and modest Victorian cottages sprang up in small enclaves. Today's residents have added their own thoughtful constructions to the river scene. From humble, rustic cabins to the grand Boldt Castle, the homes of the Thousands Islands illustrate a love affair with the river.

This book is a photographic essay on that love affair. When George Fischer and Tony Mollica asked residents of the Thousands Islands to open their homes to cameras, they came away with an inspiring collection of images that capture the essence of "A River View."

Gary DeYoung
Director of Tourism
Thousand Islands Tourism Council

THE MYSTERIOUS SUMMER RETREAT DEER ISLAND LODGE IS SAID TO BE
RESERVED FOR MEMBERS OF THE SKULL AND BONES SOCIETY.

INTRODUCTION

The Rush of '72

For more than 150 years the Thousand Islands have attracted passionate enthusiasts with their bountiful fishing, superb boating and breathtaking vistas. The St. Lawrence River is a 750-mile waterway that has as its reservoir the largest system of freshwater lakes on Earth. Reaching all the way from Lake Superior, the fully navigable waterway is nearly 2,000 miles long, connecting the heartland of North America to the Atlantic Ocean and, from there, on to the great commercial ports of the world. The St. Lawrence River begins its journey to the sea at the northeastern corner of Lake Ontario between Kingston, in Ontario, and Cape Vincent, in northern New York State. The uppermost 50 miles of the St. Lawrence River moves swiftly through a maze of nearly 2,000 islands, making it one of the most picturesque rivers anywhere.

The section of the river better known as the "Thousand Islands" begins at the river's mouth and extends for nearly 50 miles downriver. The maze of islands is so concentrated that the international boundary line between New York State and Ontario becomes indistinguishable. For local sportsmen and boaters, the islands form a series of friendly stepping stones that have blurred the border for decades. The size, shape and overall appearance of each island are remarkably varied. Some of the larger islands can still support large, productive farms and year-round residents. The picturesque islands beckon visitors to explore and enjoy the sense of quiet isolation they offer. For nearly 200 years before the arrival of Europeans, the Iroquois occupied this region and were so taken by it that they referred to it as their Garden of the Great Spirit. It was in the Thousand Islands that Hiawatha is said to have first appeared before the Confederacy of the Five Nations.

At the beginning of the nineteenth century, trappers, hunters and fishermen settled in the region. Soon, regular ferry service from Clayton's Bartlett Point to Gananoque, Ontario, was established. It didn't take long before some of the wealthier islanders created structures that were considerably more than modest summer residences. By the last quarter of the century, many of America's prominent families were discovering the Thousand Islands, and it would soon become recognized as one of the more appealing summer recreation destinations in the Northeast.

The Thousand Islands region was propelled into the national limelight when an incumbent American president agreed to spend a week's vacation in the Thousand Islands. George Pullman, one of America's high-profile industrial leaders and the developer of the rail car that bears his name, invited President Ulysses S. Grant to his Thousand Islands cottage. The President extended the invitation to include two celebrated American Civil War generals, William Sherman and Philip Sheridan. This informal gathering of illustrious vacationers became a major news event for the summer of 1872. By coincidence or by design, this celebrated visit occurred at the very same time as the National Association of Newspaper Editors annual convention at one of the Thousand Islands' hotels. Newspaper reports of the President's activities introduced millions of readers to the wonders of the region. It was also reported that, before he returned to Washington, President Grant expressed interest in purchasing nearby Friendly Island. The rapid growth period that followed the presidential visit became known as the "Rush of '72."

In 1888 George Pullman decided that it was time to replace his modest fishing lodge with a spectacular new structure. The new home would be named Castle Rest, and with its construction an era of remarkable island development commenced. Fabulous summer homes were designed by well-known architects and built on highly visible islands along the main channel. Cottage communities began to spring up along the mainland waterfront and on the shores of Wellesley Island.

Castle Rest inspired others with the means to build island castles. In 1893 tobacco merchant Charles Emery built Calumet Castle. George Boldt, of Waldorf Astoria fame,

AT SUNSET THE AMERICAN NARROWS SPAN OF THE THOUSAND ISLANDS BRIDGE
IS AN IMPRESSIVE SIGHT. THIS SPAN OF THE BRIDGE CONNECTS WELLESLEY ISLAND
TO ROUTE 81 AT COLLINS LANDING ON THE MAINLAND.

THIS BENCH APPEARS TO BE A PERFECT LOCATION FROM WHICH
TO ENJOY CARGO SHIPS FROM MAJOR PORTS AROUND THE WORLD
AS THEY PASS BY ON A BEAUTIFUL AFTERNOON.

followed suit by building his famous unfinished Boldt Castle in 1900. Singer Sewing Machine president Frederick Bourne began construction on his remarkable Dark Island Castle in 1903. The Thousand Islands had firmly established itself as the new summer playground for wealthy Americans.

The unprecedented development also spawned a wide range of service industries in the region. The small river communities began to flourish with businesses and services. Highly skilled stonemasons, carpenters, steelworkers and boatbuilders were all in demand. Lumberyards, quarries, hotels and restaurants were opened and commercial boatbuilding continued to prosper. By the turn of the century, powerboat racing was a major sport on the river. For nine consecutive years, from 1904 to 1912, the Gold Cup Trophy, boating's most prestigious national recognition for sustained speed on the water, was awarded to a member of one of the Thousand Island yacht clubs.

The stories related in this book offer a fascinating account of success and failure, of creativity and even absurdity. Many of the interesting structures of the Thousand Islands have survived for a hundred years or more, in spite of depressions, World Wars, gasoline rationing and even neglect. Even as this book is being prepared, the most famous island structure of all, Boldt Castle, continues with construction that began in 1898. George Fischer's remarkable photography captures the charm and beauty of the islands, the unusual homes, some of the rare boats and many of the enchanting details that bring out the special character of the Thousand Islands. We invite our readers to enjoy a few glimpses of life in the Thousand Islands as it is today and as it was in the past.

A VIEW ACROSS THE AMERICAN NARROWS FROM ACORN LODGE
ON WELLESLEY ISLAND TO BEAUTIFUL NEH MAHBIN,
BUILT IN 1893 ON COMFORT ISLAND.

A VIEW FROM WATER LEVEL OF THE FORMER STAFF QUARTERS ON PULLMAN ISLAND. AFTER CASTLE REST WAS RAZED IN 1956, THE STAFF QUARTERS BECAME THE ONLY RESIDENCE ON THE ISLAND.

Cottages and Castles

During the summer of 1938 President Franklin Roosevelt and Prime Minister William Mackenzie dedicated the Thousand Islands International Bridge as events in Europe and around the world were heading in catastrophic directions. The President was concerned for the safety of both the United States and Canada as the threat of war loomed. The bridge was symbolic of the strong bond between the two nations. It is also a masterpiece of design and engineering, rising 150 feet above the St. Lawrence River. The five connecting spans and their highways cover eight miles, linking the two nations and providing perhaps the best access to the Thousand Islands.

CASTLE REST

Castle Rest had the distinction of being the first castle-like structure built in the Thousand Islands. This small castle compound was built on a lovely three-and-a-half-acre island originally named Sweet Island and purchased by George Pullman in 1864. Shortly after he purchased Sweet Island, he officially changed its name to Pullman Island. A highly successful industrial entrepreneur, Pullman is best remembered for developing and manufacturing the specialized railroad sleeping cars that carry his name. From this invention alone he gained substantial wealth and founded the Pullman Palace Car Company. In 1880 he developed a model for a planned "company town" to accommodate company employees in his home state of Illinois and named it Pullman. It is now part of Chicago and continues to this day as a national historic community.

Pullman was well connected politically. As mentioned earlier, the five highly publicized days during which he entertained President Ulysses Grant and prominent Civil War Generals

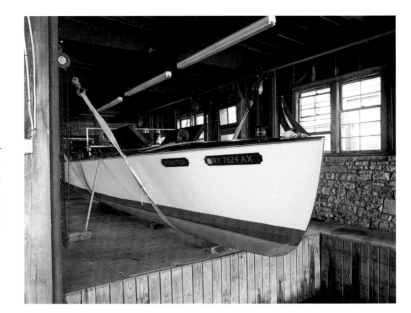

MONITOR, THE 38-FOOT HUTCHINSON BROTHERS LAUNCH THAT WAS BUILT IN 1906 IS BEING PREPARED FOR ITS 97TH SEASON ON THE RIVER. *MONITOR* CONTINUES TO RESIDE PROUDLY AT ITS ORIGINAL HOME PORT, CASTLE REST, ON PULLMAN ISLAND.

THE UPPER LEVEL OF CASTLE REST'S POWERHOUSE OFFERS A GOOD EXAMPLE OF THE DETAILED DESIGN FEATURES THAT WERE INCORPORATED INTO EVEN THE SMALLER ANCILLARY STRUCTURES OF THE PERIOD.

Sheridan and Sherman at his island retreat in 1872 proved to be a milestone in the development of the Thousand Islands. In 1888 he completed construction of a six-story, 58-room stone castle rising more than 100 feet above the river. He named it Castle Rest. The castle was complemented by additional stone buildings, including one to house a coal-fired, steam-powered electric generator, making Castle Rest the first Thousand Islands home to be fully electrified.

When Pullman died, the terms of his will stated that the island property could not be sold outside the family and that it must remain open for at least six weeks each year. Pullman's son-in-law and a former governor of Illinois, Frank Lowden, used and maintained Castle Rest throughout his lifetime. The next generation was less interested, however, and the castle was frequently unoccupied. In 1958 the Pullman heirs decided to raze the castle to reduce the nagging tax burden from the village of Alexandria Bay. After several years of negotiations, the restrictions were lifted, and Pullman Island was sold out of the family in 1971.

The new owners of Castle Rest have restored and remodeled each of the remaining ancillary buildings. One of the remaining buildings is the former servants' quarters where 22 staff members once lived. This building has been successfully transformed into a comfortable summer home without any alteration to its exterior. The magnificent granite-and-frame structure sits high above the water's edge with a four-story turret that provides a commanding view of the shipping channel. Recently a four-story frame tower in keeping with the original buildings was erected on the site of the original castle to provide additional accommodations. The new owners have also acquired Governor Lowden's 1906 38-foot launch, *Monitor*, which they use regularly each summer for touring through the islands and attending local boat shows.

TOWERS WERE POPULAR
STRUCTURES ON MANY OF
THE ISLANDS. SOMETIMES
THEY WERE USED FOR
SCENIC LOOKOUTS, TO
PROVIDE ADDITIONAL
HOUSING, TO STORE FRESH
WATER, OR AS WINDMILLS
TO PUMP WATER. THE FEW
SURVIVING TOWERS ARE
CONSIDERED VERY PRECIOUS.

THE POWERHOUSE (LEFT) AND THE STAFF QUARTERS (RIGHT) ARE TWO OF THE ORIGINAL STRUCTURES
ON PULLMAN ISLAND. THE CURRENT OWNER OCCUPIES THE STAFF QUARTERS,
WHICH SERVE AS A COMFORTABLE ISLAND RESIDENCE.

19

BLUE TOP

The unusual name Blue Top was carried over from the previous villa on this site. It may be hard to believe, but a section of the ultra-modern Blue Top was once one of George Boldt's pumphouses, which used to supply river water to several buildings nearby. Several years ago, the original stone pumphouse was adapted into a small summer residence and sold. It now serves as part of the foundation for a modern home. The owners decided that they would remove the villa, but not the original stone structure. Instead, it would be incorporated into their new home, clearly visible to boaters passing by. The original stone pumphouse walls are now walls in the ground-floor guest bedroom, providing an architectural link with the past. Blue Top is located on Wellesley Island, between the Thousand Island Club and Chalet Lodge, in the area known as Millionaire's Row. Boats travel slowly here, allowing passengers to enjoy the light and shadows that highlight the design elements of this beautiful summer home.

AN INTERESTING GUEST BEDROOM USES THE LOWER LEVEL OF BLUE TOP, TAKING ADVANTAGE OF THE MARVELOUS 100-YEAR-OLD STONE WALLS OF THE ORIGINAL BOLDT PUMPHOUSE.

A BEAUTIFUL VIEW FROM THE BALCONY OF BLUE TOP LOOKING UPRIVER TOWARD NOBBY ISLAND (LEFT) AND WELCOME ISLAND (RIGHT).

BLUE TOP IS ONE OF THE RARE CONTEMPORARY ISLAND HOMES IN THE HEART OF
MILLIONAIRE'S ROW. IT WAS BUILT ON THE STONE FOUNDATION OF ONE OF THE
BOLDT PUMPHOUSES, ONCE USED TO PUMP RIVER WATER TO HIS VARIOUS PROPERTIES.

ONE RUGGED STONE WALL OF THE ORIGINAL
BOLDT PUMPHOUSE ON WELLESLEY ISLAND
PROVIDES AN IDEAL BACKDROP ON WHICH TO
DISPLAY THE VINTAGE FISHING LURES
IN THE COTTAGE KNOWN AS BLUE TOP.

21

OAK LODGE

The summer home known as Oak Lodge is located along the American Narrows section of the river, on Wellesley Island across the channel from Keewaydin State Park. Mrs. Louise Schultz of New York City purchased the land for Oak Lodge in 1899. She was the widow of noted German chemist Carl Rudolf Schultz, who manufactured a variety of popular artificial mineral waters under the brand names "Lithia Water" and "Central Park Waters." Oak Lodge was built around 1902 for Mrs. Schultz and her family of seven daughters and four sons. The walls of the entire first story of the structure are made of irregular chunks of native granite. Fourteen absolutely massive stone pillars support the upper floor from the edge of the porch. The second floor is of the more traditional wood-frame and cedar-shingle construction. The robust structure looks like it was built to last forever. The large front porch is open and extends around three sides of the residence, providing an inviting place to sit and enjoy the abundant boating activity. The first floor of Oak Lodge has a spacious living room facing the Narrows, a formal dining room and a music room. Both the living and dining rooms were designed with large working fireplaces to provide heat on chilly evenings.

There are eleven bedrooms on the second floor and five more on the third. The abundance of sleeping accommodations was in keeping with the trend for the larger river homes at the turn of the century, but also required to accommodate the Schultz family. The exterior of Oak Lodge has remained virtually unchanged since it was constructed over a hundred years ago. It is a wonderful example of an original turn-of-the-century river residence.

LOOKING THROUGH THE WINDOW OF OAK LODGE, ONE CAN SEE THE MASSIVE STONE COLUMNS THAT SUPPORT THE UPPER FLOORS. MANY ISLAND COTTAGES FEATURE THESE ESPECIALLY HEAVY COLUMNS.

A GLIMPSE OF A LARGE FREIGHTER HEADED DOWNRIVER THROUGH THE AMERICAN NARROWS PAST OAK LODGE.

A C O R N   L O D G E

Though it is nestled in a quiet bay and surrounded by the stately oak trees of Wellesley Island, Acorn Lodge is also located on the edge of the busy American Narrows section of the St. Lawrence Seaway. It was built next to Oak Lodge in 1976 as a convenient guesthouse. It was thoughtfully planned, allowing for future expansion. This took place in 1990 and continued with a second phase completed in 2001, when the final wing was added, including a guest bedroom, an office and a formal living room. The final design succeeds in blending the old with the new so effectively that it is not apparent that the original weekend retreat has evolved into a spacious year-round home over a twenty-five year period. Attractive decks and a porch on the riverfront side of the home incorporate the natural landscape into the living space.

Acorn Lodge's owners do most of their boating in vintage classic boats. The boats are securely sheltered in their riverfront boathouse. One of their favorite boats, *Messenger*, is a superb 1929 28-foot Gar Wood runabout, a frequent trophy winner at classic boat shows.

Many island homes are expanded in stages over their lifetime as families grow, with each new generation establishing their bond with river and the islands. Acorn Lodge has grown gracefully over the years to become one of the most attractive and comfortable homes along the river.

THE SUPERB 1929 28-FOOT GAR WOOD RUNABOUT *MESSENGER* IS MOORED AT ITS WELL-PROTECTED
DOCK IN FRONT OF ACORN LODGE ON THE AMERICAN NARROWS SECTION OF THE SEAWAY.

CAREFULLY DISPLAYED ON THE CREDENZA IS A PRECISELY SCALED, MUSEUM-QUALITY MODEL OF A FAMOUS
ST. LAWRENCE ROWING SKIFF, PART OF THOUSAND ISLANDS CULTURE FOR DECADES.

JUST AFTER SUNSET, ACORN LODGE
IS FULLY ILLUMINATED IN ANTICIPATION
OF THE ARRIVAL BY BOAT OF THE
EVENING'S GUESTS FOR A FESTIVE
THOUSAND ISLANDS DINNER PARTY.

THE LIVING ROOM AND DINING
ROOM OF ACORN LODGE OPEN ONTO
A SPACIOUS DECK THAT BOASTS A
MARVELOUS VIEW OF THE AMERICAN
NARROWS.

LOCATED ON TINY HUB ISLAND, JUST ROOM ENOUGH COTTAGE
RECEIVES A LOT OF ATTENTION FROM TOUR BOATS AND MAY BE THE
MOST PHOTOGRAPHED RESIDENCE IN THE THOUSAND ISLANDS.

JUST ROOM ENOUGH

This little cottage on a tiny island that is hardly more than a shoal has been fascinating tourists and boaters along the river for decades. The sturdy structure completely covers tiny Hub Island, upon which it sits proudly with water touching on all sides. When the water level in the river is down a bit there is room for a chair or two on the slab of granite that firmly supports the house. At normal water levels, waves lap right up to the edge of the foundation. Located next door to Boldt Castle, the little cottage is the frequent recipient of tour-boat humor, with quips such as "George Boldt built this house for his mother-in-law." Frequently occupied by its owner, Just Room Enough is likely the most photographed private island home on the river.

CHIPPEWA BAY COTTAGE

Many families spend summer seasons camping in the Thousand Islands, hoping that some day they might find a suitable cottage to call their own. This family found their special cottage in Chippewa Bay during the summer of 1969. The original cottage resembled a simple California beach house. They loved the location, but the cottage required modifications, repairs and expansion. With a plan firmly in mind, they worked carefully over the years to add rooms, porches and a boathouse. Today the cottage reflects everything they need to make their visits to the river fulfilling. The cottage has become much more than just a summer home. They now enjoy spending time in the Thousand Islands in all seasons.

THE FAMILY ROOM OF THIS LOVELY CALIFORNIA-STYLE CHIPPEWA BAY COTTAGE OPENS ONTO A WONDERFUL VIEW OF THE BAY WHERE THE PRESTIGIOUS GOLD CUP POWERBOAT RACES WERE ONCE RUN.

HOPEWELL HALL

It almost seems inappropriate to refer to Hopewell Hall and other large summer homes as cottages. However, in the vernacular context of the Thousand Islands, the term "cottage" has become an acceptable idiom that is often used by island families to describe all vacation residences. William Browning built Hopewell Hall in the late 1890s after increasing his fortune making uniforms for the Union Army during the American Civil War. It was Browning who encouraged George Boldt to purchase Hart Island in 1895 as part of his personal effort to persuade more socially prominent families to become islanders. When Browning suddenly died in 1904, Boldt purchased this magnificent residence from the Browning estate. Boldt's daughter, Louise Clover, had always loved Hopewell Hall and preferred it to all of the other Boldt homes. She was especially fond of its marvelous view of the river. After she married A. Graham Miles in 1907, her father gave her Hopewell Hall as a gift. It was passed on to her daughter and remained in the family for more than ninety years.

Over the years significant changes were made to the original exterior design of Hopewell Hall. All of the third-floor dormers connected to the servants' rooms were removed several years ago. The large circular tower had its upper story removed and the pitch of the conical roof was lowered considerably. The marvelous dockhouse on the channel side was removed, as well as the dock upon which it stood. The present owners are making a superb effort to return Hopewell Hall to its days of prominence on the river.

HOPEWELL HALL SITS HIGH ABOVE THE RIVER, OFFERING A SPECTACULAR VIEW.
ONCE THE HOME OF GEORGE BOLDT'S ONLY DAUGHTER, THIS BEAUTIFUL HISTORIC HOME
AND GROUNDS STILL RECEIVE SUPERB CARE.

THE SWISS CHALET

One of several structures built by George Boldt, the Swiss Chalet on Wellesley Island was often rented to Boldt's prominent friends from Manhattan. The Chalet offers a magnificent view from its balconies, including Boldt Castle, the shipping channel, the Thousand Islands Club and several beautiful residences in the heart of Millionaire's Row. It is a short walk to the golf course, tennis courts and the superb dining room at the Thousand Islands Club. The Chalet was designed originally as a large single residence available to families as a pleasant alternative to the hotel rooms at the Thousand Islands Club. It had six master bedrooms with private baths, living room, dining room, kitchen, pantry, glass-enclosed porch and servants' quarters. Promotional literature of the period offered these instructions: "Just bring your trunks and servants." The Chalet was successfully remodeled about 20 years ago into several independent residential condominium units and each was sold to a private owner.

THE RESIDENTS OF THIS
SWISS CHALET CONDOMINIUM
ON WELLESLEY ISLAND
HAVE A WONDERFUL VIEW OF
FLORENCE ISLAND THROUGH
THE SLIDING GLASS DOORS
TO THEIR SECOND-FLOOR
BALCONY.

THE SWISS CHALET ON WELLESLEY ISLAND WAS BUILT PRIMARILY AS A RENTAL PROPERTY FOR GEORGE BOLDT'S FRIENDS. THE INTERIOR OF THE CHALET HAS BEEN REMODELED INTO HIGH-END CONDOMINIUM UNITS, BUT VERY FEW CHANGES HAVE BEEN MADE TO ITS ORIGINAL EXTERIOR.

ESTRELLITA ISLAND

Just off the northern shore of Fairyland Island is a small island called Estrellita, meaning "Little Star" in Spanish. At one time "potato chip king" Andrew S. Shuler, who made his fortune with Schuler's Potato Chips, owned the attractive lodge on Estrellita Island. A small but very important bridge connects Estrellita to Fairyland Island, where Estrellita's large boathouse and caretaker's residence are located. This cottage required two islands to complete.

ESTRELLITA (LITTLE STAR) IS A SMALL ISLAND WITH A LARGE, BEAUTIFUL HOME.
ESTRELLITA'S BOATHOUSE, ON NEARBY FAIRYLAND ISLAND,
IS REACHED VIA A CONNECTING FOOTBRIDGE.

ZAVIKON ISLAND

As tour boats approach the charming wood-frame home on Zavikon Island, passengers become aware of an attractive arched bridge spanning the 40-foot distance between Zavikon and a small islet. As the boats get closer, passengers observe a Canadian flag mounted on the north side of the bridge and an American flag on the south side. This is when tour guides proudly announce to their passengers that they are looking at "the shortest international bridge in the world," stating that Zavikon is a Canadian island and the small islet is American. It makes an interesting story and adds a bit of local color for the tourists, even if it may not be exactly correct. A study of the boundary shows that both islands are actually within Canadian waters.

THE COTTAGE ON ZAVIKON ISLAND ENJOYS A GREAT DEAL OF ATTENTION ALL SUMMER LONG FROM TOUR BOATS, WHOSE GUIDES POINT OUT THE FAMOUS BRIDGE THAT CONNECTS IT TO A SMALL ISLET CLOSE BY.

TWIN COTTAGES: BELORA AND OLYMPIA

One of the largest and most interesting of the island cottages on the river is the magnificent Belora. It has been superbly preserved as a private residence that has remained in the same family for the past 70 years. The 50-room cottage was built for Nathan Straus near the foot of Cherry Island on a rock formation high above the river. Its spacious porch wraps around the front of the cottage and provides a stunning view of the shipping channel, the cottages in the islands of Millionaire's Row and the always busy harbor in Alexandria Bay.

Nathan Straus's business partner and close friend, Abraham Abraham, built his cottage on the parcel of land right next to Belora at around the same time. The two homes were near mirror images of each other and constructed so close together that they became known among river dwellers as the Twin Cottages of Cherry Island.

In 1888 Nathan Straus and his brother, Isidor, were associated with R. H. Macy and Company. By 1896 the Straus brothers acquired total ownership of the firm and called their new family business simply Macy's. Ideally located in downtown Manhattan, Macy's grew to become the largest retail store of its type in the world.

In addition to his stake in the Macy's store, Nathan Straus was also in other partnerships with his good friend Abraham Abraham. Together they co-owned the highly regarded Abraham and Straus Store in Brooklyn that became nearly as well known as Macy's. Straus gained a national reputation for his outstanding philanthropy and role as a prominent Zionist leader. He established pasteurization stations to supply sanitary milk to the poor in 1893.

The Abraham cottage was named Olympia and located on the shipping channel side of Belora. The two large wood-frame homes presented a spectacular sight from the harbor in Alexandria Bay. After Abraham died, Straus visited the river less often and then not at all, though caretakers and gardeners maintained both homes all through the Depression.

According to a family story, around 1937 a collector of rare decanters heard that there was a desirable example among the treasured items in Belora. The collector arranged an appointment with the caretaker. Upon inspections, he quickly recognized that the decanter was, in fact, a superb piece, having four glass chambers, each providing a different choice of wine. It would be a fine addition to his collection. When he informed the caretaker that he wished to purchase the decanter, the caretaker thoughtfully explained that all the furnishings were to be included with the sale of the Twin Cottages, nothing was to be sold separately. In order to possess the rare decanter, the collector purchased the Twin Cottages and all their furnishings.

That event took place nearly seventy years ago, and today Belora is still owned by the collector's family. The prized decanter holds a prominent location in the formal dining room, where it is often used at large dinner gatherings and the story retold.

THE EARLY MORNING MIST SURROUNDS CHERRY ISLAND AND BELORA AS IT WAITS TO BE BURNED OFF BY THE RISING SUN.

THIS BEAUTIFUL HISTORIC
FOOTBRIDGE CONNECTED THE
TWIN COTTAGES ON CHERRY
ISLAND WITH TINY ISLE HELENA,
A MAN-MADE ISLET BUILT
TO HOLD THE OWNERS'
TENNIS COURT.

As the summer sun sets in the Thousand Islands, Cherry Island's magnificent Belora estate provides a striking reminder of the grand homes of the past.

Turrets supported by a single flared column contribute to the complex architecture and engineering of Belora and add a touch of magic to this wonderful Cherry Island structure.

NOBBY ISLAND

Railroad car legend George Pullman's brother James purchased Nobby Island, similar in size and a tenth of a mile downriver from his brother's island, for $40. It was an average price at the time for an island at that size and location. It was then sold to Henry Heath, who built his home here in 1872. Today Nobby Island is one of the jewels of the river, nestled in the midst of Millionaire's Row, with a beautifully maintained vintage home plus an attractive stick-style cottage guesthouse. The small island also features a large boat port, extensive gardens and a beautiful stone bridge connecting Nobby to a tiny islet at its head.

THIS CLASSIC NOBBY ISLAND RESIDENCE SITS HIGH ABOVE A BEAUTIFUL FLOWER GARDEN NEAR THE WATER'S EDGE. THE ISLAND GARDENS OFFER BURSTS OF VIVID COLOR FOR PASSING BOATERS TO ENJOY.

OPAWAKA LODGE

Until 1960 the magnificent Opawaka Lodge was the island home of Congressman Joseph Hendrix Himes. The home is built on Dashwood Island, in Canada, and is often called the "House of Seven Gables" by tour guides. The reference to seven gables is likely a misplaced allusion to the seven dormers facing the front of the house. Himes, whose fortune was produced in the Pittsburgh steel industry, was an Ohio congressman and Washington resident who summered in Canada. According to author Paul Malo, Opawaka Lodge "was said to have been the largest residence on a Canadian island when it was built in 1900. The white house with its very long porch stretches along the top of a rocky cliff. It's not at all rustic, but is large, not overly ostentatious, and especially attractive."

POWERFUL AIRBOATS BECOME THE ONLY PRACTICAL WAY TO TRAVEL OVER THE RIVER DURING THE WINTER MONTHS WHEN BOTH ICE AND OPEN WATER ARE COMMONPLACE.

WELL-MEANING TOUR-BOAT GUIDES OFTEN REFER TO BEAUTIFUL OPAWAKA LODGE ON CANADA'S DASHWOOD ISLAND AS THE "HOUSE OF SEVEN GABLES." THE ERROR IS LIKELY THE RESULT OF ITS SEVEN PROMINENT DORMERS.

CALUMET TOWER

Charles Emery's tobacco products business grew steadily from a small family operation to a major corporation. Emery's patented cigarette machine brought down production costs and raised profits dramatically for his firm, Goodwin & Company. Goodwin & Company and four other leading tobacco firms combined in 1890 to form the giant American Tobacco Company, adding millions of dollars to Emery's wealth.

Emery first visited the Thousand Islands while on vacation in 1881. The following summer he purchased Powder Horn Island, directly opposite the village of Clayton. He renamed the island Calumet, a reference to the Native American peace pipe and an indirect connection to the tobacco on which his fortune was based. By the summer of 1883, the Emerys had designed and built an attractive cottage that they enjoyed for ten summers. But deeply impressed by George Pullman's Castle Rest on Alexandria Bay, Emery decided to build a new home on Calumet Island that would provide Clayton with a structure equally as imposing.

The new Emery residence was one of the truly great island structures constructed on the river. Emery used Potsdam sandstone for his new residence, which he said was designed and constructed "to last forever." It was the first large castle-type home that ships would see as they headed downriver from Lake Ontario. Alongside the castle, a tower was erected with a magnificent view in all directions.

Unfortunately, the castle was heavily damaged by fire in 1957. The remains were so unstable that they had to be removed, but the original Emery cottage used as the care-taker's residence survived. It is a superb wood-frame structure that serves as the present owner's residence. Ironically, Emery's son and grandson always preferred this dwelling to the castle.

THE WOODEN FRAME
TOWER ON CALUMET
ISLAND HAS BEEN
SUPERBLY MAINTAINED
AS ONE OF FINE
ORIGINAL STRUCTURES
FROM THE GLORY DAYS
OF CHARLES EMERY
AND HIS FASCINATING
CALUMET CASTLE.

THE IMAGE OF A PASSING FREIGHTER, SEEN THROUGH
SKELDING LODGE'S LARGE CIRCULAR WINDOW, IS A REGULAR
REMINDER OF LIFE ALONG THE ST. LAWRENCE SEAWAY.

SKELDING LODGE

This comfortable, modern year-round home is located along the American Narrows section in an older area know as St. Lawrence Park. Just a short distance from shore, the water depth drops quickly, allowing seagoing freighters to travel unusually close. This remarkable water depth also provides Skelding's owners with unusual fishing opportunities without leaving their property. Looking upriver the owners have a perfect view of the majestic American span of the Thousand Islands Bridge. The lodge's large circular window often captures a magical moment when a passing freighter is perfectly framed within its circumference. The American Narrows is a busy waterway, but it never lacks for excitement when a cargo ship, one of the largest moving objects on Earth, steers silently past your front door.

THOUSAND ISLAND PARK

Religious denominations discovered that the Thousand Islands provided a place where small summer communities of followers and their families could spend a few summer weeks enjoying the scenic beauty and at the same time strengthening their beliefs. A Methodist group established a cottage community called Thousand Island Park on the southwestern tip of Wellesley Island in 1875. The founders imposed strict regulations that prohibited dancing, alcoholic beverages, and the arrival or departure of boats on Sundays. Many summer visitors found this too restrictive and just too dull. To compensate, the founders arranged musical performances at the large open-air tabernacle. Over time, the restrictions were lifted, and it has become one of most enjoyable and beautiful island communities on the river.

The typical cottage at Thousand Island Park was built just above ground level. Virtually every cottage has a large wraparound front porch. French doors provide good ventilation and plenty of natural light. The abundance of decorative fretwork, commonly referred to as "gingerbread," helps give the community its charming appearance. The most popular architecture in Thousand Island Park is the stick-style cottage. The buildings are individually owned in Thousand Island Park, but the land upon which the cottages are built is still owned by the corporate association, which has its own governing board.

NEARLY ALL OF THE
VINTAGE COTTAGES IN
THOUSAND ISLAND PARK
FEATURE WONDERFULLY
DETAILED FRETWORK.
THE ORNAMENTATION ON
SWEETHEART COTTAGE,
WITH ITS WHIMSICAL
HEART-SHAPED PORCH, IS
DELIGHTFULLY DISTINCTIVE
AND OFTEN BRINGS A
SMILE TO PASSERSBY.

THE SECOND-FLOOR PORCHES IN THOUSAND ISLAND PARK ARE POPULAR PLACES FROM WHICH TO WATCH SHIPS, READ A BOOK OR ENJOY A MID-AFTERNOON NAP IN THE FRESH AIR.

ORNATE FRETWORK IS A CHARMING ARCHITECTURAL TRADITION IN THOUSAND ISLAND PARK.

NEARLY ALL OF THE COTTAGES IN
THOUSAND ISLAND PARK OFFER
DELIGHTFUL ARCHITECTURAL DETAILS.
SOME STRUCTURES ARE ALSO QUITE
LARGE, FEATURING EXTENSIVE PORCHES
AND EVEN LARGE TOWERS.

COMFORTABLE FRONT, SIDE AND
WRAPAROUND PORCHES ARE AMONG
THE MOST IMPORTANT FEATURES OF
TRADITIONAL THOUSAND ISLANDS
COTTAGES. NOWHERE ARE PORCHES
MORE POPULAR THAN IN THOUSAND
ISLAND PARK, WHERE PORCH-VISITING
IS A WAY OF LIFE.

COZY PORCHES TRIMMED WITH INTERESTING FRETWORK AND FURNISHED WITH COMFORTABLE OLD WICKER FURNITURE PRESENT INVITING LOCATIONS FOR FRIENDLY HOSPITALITY ALL SUMMER.

BICYCLES, THE MOST POPULAR FORM OF LAND TRANSPORTATION AMONG THE SUMMER FAMILIES OF THOUSAND ISLAND PARK, OFTEN FIND PORCHES TO BE THE MOST SUITABLE PLACES TO PARK.

THERE ARE AN INCREASING
NUMBER OF YEAR-ROUND
RESIDENTS IN THOUSAND
ISLAND PARK, WHERE THE
WINTERS ARE BEAUTIFUL BUT
CHALLENGING FOR A SUMMER
COMMUNITY.

CASA BLANCA

Casa Blanca may be one of the most photographed private homes in the Thousand Islands. It is located on picturesque Cherry Island overlooking the main shipping channel of the St. Lawrence Seaway. Tour boats pass close by to point out this beautiful home's architectural features, extensive gardens and row of fierce-looking gargoyles. A delightful wraparound porch, a large solarium and eye-catching towers nicely complement the main structure.

It was built for the Pullman family in 1881 and called Melrose Lodge. In 1897 Luis Marx purchased the modest home at an estate auction because he loved Cherry Island

ONE OF SEVERAL FIERCE GARGOYLES THAT HAVE BEEN PERMANENTLY STATIONED ON THE SEAWALL OUTSIDE CASA BLANCA TO WARD OFF POSSIBLE INTRUDERS.

and its splendid location on the shipping channel, near both the Yacht Club and Alexandria Bay. It was purchased just in time to be used for the wedding of Marx's daughter. Inspired by the Chicago World's Fair, Marx installed a large, lighted fountain that was illuminated every night, to the delight of passing steamboats. The original lodge has been successfully assimilated as the rear wing of the present, much larger Casa Blanca.

Casa Blanca has an interesting residential boathouse on the river, a two-story, wood-frame structure with a three-bedroom residence on the second floor. Each room is paneled with natural knot-free fir beaded boards on all walls and the ceilings. A small balcony overlooks the Edgewood Channel and the attractive homes recently built along the shore of the mainland. The lower level features four 30-foot boat slips with a dock running the full length of the structure.

CHERRY ISLAND'S BEAUTIFUL CASA BLANCA IS ONE OF THE MOST PHOTOGRAPHED OF ALL ISLAND HOMES.

FREDRICK BOURNE'S FAMILY WAS CONVINCED THAT HE WAS BUILDING A MODEST FISHING
AND HUNTING LODGE UNTIL HE SURPRISED THEM WITH BEAUTIFUL SINGER CASTLE DURING THE
SUMMER OF 1906. IT IS ONE OF THE LAST OF THE GREAT ST. LAWRENCE RIVER CASTLES,
AND IN 2003 IT WAS MADE AVAILABLE FOR GUIDED TOURS.

THE TOWERS ON DARK ISLAND
(SINGER CASTLE)

Frederick G. Bourne, president of the Singer Sewing Machine factory and commodore of the New York Yacht Club, became a prominent force in the development of the Thousand Islands. It is said that he promised his family an island retreat but referred to his plans as a "shooting and fishing shack." Mischievously, Bourne kept details of his plan a secret from his family. The new castle was ready by the summer of 1906, and we can only imagine how the Bourne family felt when they first glimpsed the castle on Dark Island. As their boat drew closer, there was no way to hide the towering structure rising high above the seven-acre island in the middle of the St. Lawrence River. Looming ahead was the magnificent new, fully furnished, fully staffed castle of 33 rooms.

Bourne officially named his new island residence The Towers. The island is identified on the navigational charts as Dark Island. Renowned architect Ernest Flagg designed the castle and perhaps each of the seven ancillary buildings. Flagg was also the architect selected by Bourne to design the Singer Building, New York City's tallest building at the time. The castellated stone structure took two years to build using local pink granite from George Boldt's Oak Island quarry, a short distance upriver from Dark Island. The castle is positioned on a great stone ledge overlooking the main shipping channel. Its location and prominent towers help make the structure appear even larger than its actual dimensions. Flagg's ingenious design tends to favor Scottish-style castles, in spite of the decidedly Spanish influence of its bright red-tile roofs.

THIS INTERESTING WROUGHT-IRON LIGHT FIXTURE ON THE EXTERIOR WALL IS ANOTHER EXAMPLE OF THE SPECIAL ORNAMENTATION CREATED ESPECIALLY FOR THE TOWERS.

A SUPERB VIEW OF THE TOWERS' NATIVE PINK GRANITE, SHOWING THE MASSIVE TURRET
AND THE NUMEROUS LARGE WINDOWS THAT PROVIDE ABUNDANT NATURAL LIGHT.

The massive entry hall measures 36 by 33 feet and conveys a mood traditionally associated with ancient castles. At the far end of the hall is an arched opening under which are wide stone steps that lead to the drawing room, a chamber measuring 36 feet square, with a huge pink marble fireplace adorned by one of Mr. Bourne's prized hunting trophies, a mounted elk. The large room also features three separate alcoves with Pullman-style window seats for quiet conversations or viewing the river. Off the southwest corner of the drawing room, located inside the stone turret, is Mr. Bourne's circular office. At the far end of the drawing room is the glass-enclosed loggia with its own large fireplace.

The formal dining room is 30 by 20 feet, with natural-finished, raised oak paneling, an oak-beamed ceiling and a massive marble fireplace. Family and guests are served from a large butler's pantry and partially hidden serving room. Food preparation takes place in large kitchens on the main floor using the dumbwaiter delivery system.

The third floor is primarily devoted to several large bedroom suites. The generous servants' quarters, with five bedrooms, are located on the main floor in the wing devoted to castle services. In this wing are two kitchens, the laundry, storage facilities and the furnace room with its 5,000-gallon fuel tank for the steam heating system. The large family library, 32 by 18 feet, is located just off the great entry hall on the main floor. Flagg incorporated a series of secret passageways and hidden spiral stairs inside the residence that add to the authentic mystique often associated with ancient castles.

The island has several additional buildings, including a stunning five-story pink granite Clock Tower. The massive clocks, on all four sides, are 12 feet in diameter with 6-foot hands and provide the sweet sounds of Westminster chimes

THIS EXOTIC DOOR HANDLE IS AN INTERESTING EXAMPLE OF THE SPECIAL HARDWARE MADE EXCLUSIVELY FOR THE TOWERS ON DARK ISLAND.

THE TOWERS' ARCHITECT WANTED TO FLOOD
THE BREAKFAST ROOM WITH AS MUCH
NATURAL LIGHT AS POSSIBLE.

on the hour. An elevated stone passageway connects the Clock Tower to both the South Boathouse and the castle's great entry hall. This thoughtfully planned enclosed corridor provides arriving guests with a fully protected entry into the castle in the event of unpleasant weather. Originally the island had an icehouse that was capable of holding two tons of ice harvested during the winter to last through the summer season.

Bourne loved boats and served as commodore of both the Thousand Islands Yacht Club and the New York Yacht Club. He owned several small boats and a hundred-foot steam yacht. His two large boathouses on the north and south shores of the island could accommodate all his boats and provide sleeping quarters for his crew in nine bedrooms. At the foot of the island in a naturally formed bay is a special aircraft hanger for Bourne's personal floatplane.

When Bourne died in 1919 the castle was bequeathed to his daughter, who continued to enjoy the castle for several years. After her death in 1962 the property was owned by the LaSalle Military Academy in Bourne's hometown of Oakdale, Long Island, New York. After three years of ownership, the Academy sold the property. It remained in private ownership until recently, when it was sold to a foreign corporation with elaborate plans for transportation to and from Dark Island and guided tours of the buildings and grounds. In decades past, the castle has been called The Towers, Jorstad Castle and Dark Island Castle. The new owners plan to identify it as Singer Castle, to honor the great business enterprise that provided Bourne with the means to build it.

In contrast to the larger Boldt Castle, Dark Island Castle provides the warmer feeling, having been finished, furnished and lived in by a family who enjoyed it for decades.

THE LARGE BREAKFAST ROOM ON THE SECOND FLOOR OF THE TOWERS OPENS ONTO A LARGE TERRACE THAT
OVERLOOKS THE MAIN SHIPPING CHANNEL AND CHIPPEWA BAY IN THE DISTANCE.

THE TOWERS' DRAWING ROOM
MEASURES 36 FEET SQUARE AND
HAS A PINK-MARBLE FIREPLACE
ADORNED WITH ONE OF BOURNE'S
HUNTING TROPHIES.

THE TOWERS' FORMAL DINING ROOM
IS LOCATED ON THE SECOND FLOOR
AND FEATURES ENGLISH WALNUT
RAISED PANELS, A FULLY BEAMED
CEILING AND A LARGE FIREPLACE.

THERE IS A WONDERFUL VIEW OF THE SHIPPING CHANNEL, THE CLOCK TOWER AND THE SOUTH BOATHOUSE FROM INSIDE ONE OF THE THREE COZY ALCOVES IN THE TOWERS' DRAWING ROOM.

THE TEMPERATURE-CONTROLLED WINE STORAGE ROOM IS ADJACENT TO THE ENTRANCE HALL ON THE MAIN FLOOR IN THE TOWERS.

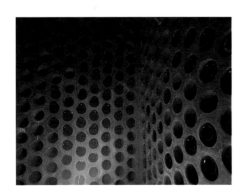

ON THE ROCKS

Wonderful new dwellings are still being constructed along the river. On the Rocks is an example of a new residence that captures the essence of the river culture superbly. The location is the American Narrows section of Wellesley Island, on a parcel of land that has been in the owner's family since the late 1800s. The owner spent summers on the river throughout his life and fully understands the features necessary to have a comfortable, secure, all-season home along the St. Lawrence. The owner and the architect demonstrated a solid grasp of traditional river styles and a sound approach to what would work well in this location. The owner describes it as "a river design home with porches, lots of windows, several rooms with cathedral ceilings and exquisite detailing with pine, mahogany, cherry, fir, and beech woods." The use of indigenous materials such as the nine tons of granite quarried in Alexandria Bay strengthened the relationship of the house to the site. The colors and textures of the house reflect the surrounding woods, rocks and mosses.

COLORFUL BIRDHOUSES PROVIDE INTERESTING SHELTERS FOR THE WIDE RANGE OF SONGBIRDS THAT POPULATE THE LUSH, GREEN ISLANDS OF THE ST. LAWRENCE RIVER VALLEY.

The house is designed around a spacious kitchen in the center of the home, with clear views to the main channel of the river through the screen porch on the front of the house. The kitchen has granite countertops and maple cabinets that feature original river scenes painted by artist Michael Ringer. Large overhangs and built-in shades provide enough protection to allow the screened porch to be used for summer dining. The porch floors are finished mahogany with natural beaded fir on the ceiling. Above this porch, on the second level, are two more screen porches outside each of two bedrooms. There are four bedrooms on the second floor, all with superb views. Two of the bedrooms have cathedral ceilings with arched wooden trusses.

The design of On the Rocks combines open spaces with traditional forms. Clear spans and expansive windows were possible through the use of engineered lumber. The house is positioned to take advantage of the river views, yet from the river the full view of the house is well hidden. On the Rocks is a thoughtfully designed river cottage that is just as comfortable on a crisp winter's day as it is in mid-summer.

NATIVE PINK-GRANITE WALLS WITH BLUESTONE CAPS FRAME THE STONE STEPS THAT LEAD TO THE MAIN ENTRANCE OF ON THE ROCKS, A YEAR-ROUND HOME ON WELLESLEY ISLAND DESIGNED BY LOCAL ARCHITECT BILL GRATER AND BUILT IN 1999.

AN ABUNDANCE OF TALL PINES AND
OAKS SHELTER THE SCREENED PORCH
THAT FACES THE SEAWAY JUST BELOW
ON THE ROCKS. THE PORCH PROVIDES
AN INVITING EXTENSION OF THE
LIVING SPACE AND IS FREQUENTLY
USED FOR SUMMER DINING.

INSIDE ON THE ROCKS WE FIND
AN INVITING GREAT ROOM WITH
COMFORTABLE WICKER FURNITURE,
A RAISED-HEARTH FIREPLACE AND
ABUNDANT NATURAL LIGHT.

THE CATHEDRAL CEILING IN THE MASTER BEDROOM OF ON THE ROCKS IS ACCENTUATED
BY THE ARCHED WOODEN TRUSSES, PROVIDING A REFRESHING SENSE OF THE SPACE.

THE ATTRACTIVE HALF-HULL MODEL OF THE
FAMOUS 1910 RACEBOAT *NIGHT RIDER*
IS MOUNTED PROMINENTLY ON THE
PORCH WALL OF ON THE ROCKS.

B O L D T   C A S T L E

George Boldt was just 13 years old when he left his home in Prussia to journey alone to America. All he had was his intelligence, a willingness to work and the ability to please others. His remarkable career in the hospitality industry began in the kitchen of New York's Merchant's Exchange Hotel and involved stints at the Arlington Hotel, Parker's Restaurant and Cornwall-on-the-Hudson. After two successful years in Cornwall, he moved to Philadelphia and the exclusive Philadelphia Club. Club manager William Kehrer took an immediate liking to Boldt and the following year, 1877, Boldt married Kehrer's daughter, Louise, then 15.

By the time he was 30, Boldt had become manager of Philadelphia's Petrie's French Restaurant. After a few years he leased it from its owners, then secured financial backing to purchase and transform the four-story building into an exclusive hotel called the Hotel Bellevue. Members of the prestigious Philadelphia Club and Clover Club selected Boldt's Bellevue as their location of choice. Seven years after opening the Bellevue, Boldt

purchased the shabby six-story hotel directly across the street and lavishly remodeled it as the Stratford Hotel. The two hotels enjoyed an equally fine reputation and were the first choice of prominent visitors to Philadelphia, including the extremely wealthy William Waldorf Astor.

Astor wanted to construct a glamorous new hotel on the site of his 33rd Street mansion in Manhattan. The success of the venture would depend on the skill of its manager, and the only choice acceptable to Astor was George Boldt. Boldt made it clear he must have total control and insisted that his compensation be based solely on a profit-sharing arrangement. The agreement was

BOLDT CASTLE FEATURES MANY REMINDERS OF THE BOLDT FAMILY. THIS BEAUTIFUL LEADED-GLASS PANEL SHOWS THEIR TRADITIONAL STAG, THE HEART AND THE UNIQUE "B" WITH A PAIR OF CLOVERS.

settled, with Astor owning the land and the building and Boldt as the lessee. The 450-room Waldorf was completed and ready for occupancy in the spring of 1893. Boldt was prepared to give New York City a place of dazzling luxury, catering to New York's most prominent families by making dining out at the Waldorf a way of life.

A year after the Waldorf Hotel opened, Boldt visited the Thousand Islands as guest of honor at Thousand Island Yacht Club in Alexandria Bay. Boldt loved the islands and by the following summer had purchased his Hart Island home. Within weeks, building and remodeling commenced at a feverish pace. The original Hart house was expanded to a reported 56 rooms, with a tower that reached two stories above the roof. Boldt referred to illustrations of an old Rhine River castle for the construction of a similar structure at the head of the Hart Island. The new building was to serve as a recreation center for guests and the Boldt children and would be known as Alster Tower, or simply "the playhouse."

The expansion of the Hart house had hardly finished when Boldt was inspired to build a much larger stone chateau. It would be the largest private residence of its type in the Thousand Islands and one of the largest in North America, with a hundred rooms.

Close to Alster Tower, Boldt wanted a formal entrance where small craft could pass under an arch into a quite lagoon. From the lagoon, guests could walk up elaborate stone steps to chateau's main entrance. He also decided that the island needed to be reshaped slightly to resemble a heart, allowing him to rename it "Heart Island," in keeping with the romantic theme of the chateau.

On a rocky shoal at the foot of the island, Boldt built a powerhouse with a chiming clock tower. The tower was connected to Heart Island by an arched stone bridge. In 1936 the powerhouse's wooden roof was destroyed when it accidentally caught fire during a fireworks display. The roofless building was left exposed to the weather for nearly 60 years. Somehow the building endured the decades of exposure, and the roof has now been accurately replaced as part of a Thousand Islands Bridge Authority restoration program. The powerhouse has four roof spires and on the tallest tower are the four illuminated clock faces. The lower level was equipped with three powerful dynamos, and the upper floor provided living quarters for the engineer and machinist.

The architects and Boldt originally referred the owner's residence as "the chateau," but today it is known as "the castle." The castle is an immense building, 150 feet long and 115 feet wide at its base and soaring six stories high. Although it was a personal residence, the scale was nearly that of a small hotel, which was what Boldt knew best.

The first-floor layout provided for a reception room, dining room, kitchen, butler's pantry, maids' and servants' dining room, billiard room, library, office for Mr. Boldt and a ballroom. The second floor has the Boldt family suites and several guest apartments, each with private bath and their own fireplaces. There are more guest apartments on the third floor. The fourth floor has servants' quarters, guest rooms, a photographic dark room, reading room, an observation deck and a 10,000-gallon rainwater tank. Above this level are tower rooms and spectacular lookouts. The basement level has an indoor

A CLOSER VIEW OF THE UPPER LEVEL OF THE LOOKOUT TOWER ON THE RESIDENTIAL UNIT OF THE BOLDT CASTLE YACHT HOUSE SHOWS THE ATTENTION GIVEN TO ARCHITECTURAL DETAIL.

swimming pool with plans for dressing rooms and a lounge. Plans for the service section of the basement included a wine cellar, ice storage, a large bakery, a boiler room to produce steam heat for the house and an enclosed service passage under the terrace to bring supplies and baggage into the residence virtually unnoticed.

Work on the chateau began in 1900 with the best craftsmen available. No detail was too small nor expense too great. George and Louise were involved in every aspect of the design and looked forward to the task of selecting fixtures, furnishings and art from various parts of the world for their chateau.

After nearly four years of work, the Boldts' island escape was almost completed when Mrs. Boldt, who had been in delicate health for some time, died on January 7, 1904. She was just 41 years old. George Boldt immediately halted work on the project. Nearly everyone believed that the stoppage was simply a respectful pause in construction. However, Boldt never lifted the stoppage order, and legend has it that he never set foot on Heart Island again. For the final 12 years of his life, Boldt simply stepped away and allowed time, neglect and the elements to have their way with the Heart Island compound.

Now, a century later, Boldt Castle visitors frequently end their tour vexed by questions as to why such a resourceful and successful man would abandon such a conspicuous project when completion was so close. We will never know the true reason, but as noted Boldt historian Paul Malo points out in his book, *Boldt Castle*: "Paradoxically, it was George Boldt's decision to abandon the Castle, that saved it. The legendary romance of Heart Island has intrigued millions of visitors, providing for its maintenance and restoration. Had Boldt finished building his Castle, its life would have been finished. Today, it lives in the imagination of the public."

THIS VIEW OF BOLDT CASTLE BELOW A FULL MOON ON A SILENT WINTER'S EVENING PROVIDES SHARP CONTRAST TO THE BUSY WATERWAYS OF SUMMER WHEN TENS OF THOUSANDS OF CURIOUS VISITORS FLOCK TO THE ISLAND.

A VIEW OF BOLDT CASTLE'S COMPLEX
ROOF DESIGN CLEARLY ILLUSTRATES
OF THE SKILL OF THE ARCHITECTS,
ENGINEERS AND BUILDERS WHO WORKED
ON THIS MAGNIFICENT STRUCTURE.

THE BOLDT POWERHOUSE AND CLOCK
TOWER WERE CONSTRUCTED ENTIRELY ON A
LARGE SHOAL SO THAT THEY APPEAR
TO BE EMERGING FROM THE WATER.
THE FOUR CLOCK FACES LOCATED IN THE
TALLEST TOWER KEEP PERFECT TIME
AND CHIME ON THE HOUR.

THIS AERIAL VIEW OF BOLDT CASTLE SURROUNDED BY COLORFUL FALL FOLIAGE ALSO SHOWS
THE CHATEAU'S COMPLEX ROOF WITH ITS DORMERS, TOWERS AND LEDGES.

Gazing up the grand staircase from the large reception hall to the second floor, visitors get a sense of what the castle might have been like if it had been finished as planned. The detailing in the second- and third-floor ceilings has been carefully restored.

The vaulted stained-glass skylight floods each floor around the grand staircase, through the rotunda to the reception hall, with natural sunlight.

On a fall afternoon in Boldt Castle, flaming logs remove the chill just below the grand staircase where the family emblem is set in the marble floor.

THE PINK-GRANITE BOATHOUSE AT SINGER CASTLE IS 100 FEET IN LENGTH AND FEATURES
A SERIES OF BEAUTIFULLY ARCHED WINDOWS TO PROVIDE ABUNDANT NATURAL LIGHT TO THE INTERIOR.
THE MASSIVE STRUCTURE WAS DESIGNED TO SUCCESSFULLY STAND UP TO THE STRONG SWEEP
OF WIND COMMON TO THIS OPEN STRETCH OF THE RIVER.

Boathouses and Houseboats

Boathouses in the Thousand Islands region have to contend with freezing water, the weight of heavy snowfalls and the incredible power of moving ice, not to mention the constant battering of waves during the boating season and the stress caused when the boats are lifted in their slips. It's a tough existence, and the boathouses that survive 75 or more years are deserving of whatever it takes to keep them properly maintained. Features such as proper water depth close to shore, a shelf of bedrock under the structure, natural protection from ice floe damage and limited exposure to destructive waves are all important considerations if a boathouse is to endure.

A boathouse takes on a magnetic appeal when it includes living quarters. Residing and sleeping over the water is almost like living on a large cruise ship. In recent years the construction of boathouses with full living accommodations has unfortunately become a thing of the past. Current building restrictions prohibit the construction of residential boathouses on most lakes and rivers due to environmental considerations related to plumbing. This is why older boathouses with residential accommodations are considered to be irreplaceable possessions and are maintained with tender, loving care.

THE BRIGHT-RED ROOF, DORMER FRETWORK AND SAILBOAT CUTOUTS
IN THE SHUTTERS OF THE EDGEWATER BOATHOUSE ADD UNIQUE
DECORATIVE TOUCHES TO THE VINTAGE ISLAND STRUCTURE.

EDGEWATER

This charming little boathouse has earned its keep for more than a hundred years on the shores of Cherry Island. It is on the parcel of land where Stuyvesant Lodge was built for Reverend Rockwell in 1855. For many years the second floor of the boathouse was a well-equipped machine shop serving the needs of the island homes and the owners' boats. When additional living quarters were required some 60 years ago for domestic staff, the upper floor was remodeled to provide a complete residence. The lower level incorporates utilities, a laundry, a small shop and a 22-foot boat slip. The upper level has a sleeping porch that extends over the full width of the building, a combination living and dining room, a full kitchen, two bedrooms and a large open porch. The remodeled structure was called Edgewater, and it has remained essentially the same ever since.

Edgewater is anchored along the shore to a stone wall and supported along each side by three large cedar cribs filled with granite to provide solid footing. Each fall the family runabout is lifted in its slip and stored through the winter season on three wooden beams.

FOR NEARLY A HUNDRED YEARS EDGEWATER, A CHARMING LIVE-IN BOATHOUSE ON CHERRY ISLAND, HAS STOOD THE TEST OF TIME. ITS IDEAL LOCATION PROTECTS IT FROM THE PREVAILING WINDS, WAVES AND ICE FLOES, MAKING IT A PERFECT SHELTER FOR A CLASSIC RUNABOUT.

BOLDT YACHT HOUSE

One of the truly remarkable structures of the Thousand Islands is the yacht house that George Boldt built to accommodate his fleet. Noted historian Roger Lucas determined that Boldt owned as many as 60 watercraft, including skiffs, yachts, runabouts and workboats. Some of the more noteworthy watercraft in Boldt's vast fleet included the 114-foot houseboat *La Duchesse*; his three steam yachts, the 102-foot *Louise*, the 80-foot *Presto* and the 81-foot *Clover*; a sailing yacht named *Cocoa*; and several powerful race boats. The yacht house is an incredibly large, steel-framed, wooden structure that presents the appearance of a great cathedral built over the water. Three of its four slips were designed specifically for Boldt's large yachts. At the entrance to each yacht slip were pairs of huge, motorized hinged doors that extended from the surface of the water to nearly the peak of the roof. The remarkably tall openings were required to accommodate the heights of the tall masts on each yacht. In addition, the roof over the large center slip was equipped with a giant rooftop cupola. Inside the yacht house and under the cupola was an equally large funnel that could be lowered over a yacht's smokestack while it remained in its slip. A member of the yacht's crew would operate a crank handle at the dock level to operate this simple yet ingenious device. By lowering the funnel, the steam engine crew could fire-up the yacht's boilers to normal operating temperatures while the yacht was still in its slip. This system prepared the yacht for service without any accumulation of smoke inside the yacht house.

Large coal storage bins provided a ready supply of fuel for the steam yachts. Attached to the yacht house is a dwelling with room enough for an entire yacht crew, allowing them to be available on short notice.

A fully equipped shop with boatbuilding capabilities was located just beyond the forward end of the yacht slips. Many of the famous P.D.Q. race boats that Boldt's son-in-law A. Graham Miles raced in Gold Cup competition were constructed in this shop. Located along the length of each slip are a series of screw jacks that connect to steel beams at the bottom of the slip. The jacks provide a simple but effective system for raising vessels out of the water for service or storage, eliminating the need for chains and other lifting devices. The screw jacks still operate effectively to lift heavy boats after all these years. Despite the size of the yacht house and its position over the water, it is an unusually attractive structure. Visitors may tour it and see several boats from Boldt's original fleet. The seven-story Boldt yacht house is more than 100 years old and continues to defy time and the elements, standing straight, tall and secure on its deepwater foundation on the edge of Fern Island.

THE BOLDT YACHT HOUSE IS ONE OF THE GREAT TREASURES OF THE THOUSAND ISLANDS. BUILT AT THE TURN OF THE CENTURY FOR GEORGE BOLDT'S LARGE STEAM YACHTS, IT ALSO INCLUDES A RESIDENCE FOR HIS YACHT CREW. THIS REMARKABLE STEEL-FRAMED WOODEN STRUCTURE STILL STANDS STRAIGHT AND TALL ON ITS DEEP-WATER FOOTINGS.

THE ABUNDANT ROOF
DORMERS PROVIDE
PLENTY OF NATURAL
LIGHT INSIDE THE
HUGE BOLDT
YACHT HOUSE.

THE SPECIAL CUPOLA ON THE ROOF OF THE BOLDT YACHT HOUSE SO EFFECTIVELY REMOVED
THE SMOKE GENERATED BY BOLDT'S STEAM YACHT THAT THE CREW COULD LET THE BOILER
REACH OPERATING TEMPERATURES INSIDE THE STRUCTURE.

LA DUCHESSE

Shortly after George Boldt decided to remove the original E. Kirke Hart house from his island and replace it with a new chateau of grand proportions, he took delivery of his fabulous new houseboat, *La Duchesse*. It was 114 feet long with a beam of 26 feet and cost of $175,000 in 1900. It was intended to provide the Boldt family with an alternate place to live while construction was underway for the new chateau.

Edward J. Noble, C.E.O. of the highly successful Life Saver Candy Company, acquired most of Boldt's Thousand Island properties from the Boldt estate. His acquisitions included the *La Duchesse*. In 1943 Andrew McNally III, the former chairman of the Rand McNally Publishing Company of Chicago and a lifelong islander, purchased *La Duchesse* from Noble. At the time of the purchase, the houseboat was partially sunk at its dock, its mahogany hull leaking and in need of attention. Repairs were made and in 1958 a completely new steel hull constructed by the Hutchinson Boat Works in Alexandria Bay provided a lasting structure for the magnificent houseboat. Andrew McNally saved *La Duchesse*, and she became his preferred summer residence, moored at the McNally family compound on Isle Royal and Wellesley Island.

The accommodations on *La Duchesse* are outstanding. The first level has a large full-service kitchen with an eating area and two staff cabins with bath. Amidships there is a large dining room with an operating fireplace. Continuing aft through a center hall, there are six guest cabins, three on each side, all with washstands. The cabins and the hallway are covered with highly detailed, raised-panel, solid Honduras mahogany with a light satin varnish finish. There are also two full bathrooms with tubs and showers for the guest cabins. The ceiling height is a full eight feet throughout the interior. The second level is reached via a stairway of Honduras mahogany from the dining room to the grand salon. At the forward end of the second level is the owner's large cabin with an office, an open porch, a private bath and abundant storage. The cabin walls are also natural raised-panel Honduras mahogany. Aft of this is the grand salon, with a Tiffany stained-glass skylight located above the Steinway upright piano, a working fireplace, and beautifully detailed raised paneling throughout. Mounted on the paneled wall alongside the fireplace is a half-hull scale model of *Night Rider*, one of the McNally's classic Leyare race boats.

Perhaps, one of *La Duchess*'s most impressive features is the 50-by-20-foot screened promenade deck. This attractive deck is furnished with gracious white wicker chairs and sofas and fragrant flowers grown in the McNally garden. The deck sole is clear-finished long-grain spruce. The promenade deck also provided a wonderful natural floor for dancing during gala social gatherings. Since its first days *La Duchesse* has always had fresh

THE MAGNIFICENT HOUSEBOAT *LA DUCHESSE* ALONG WITH THE FAMILY'S
25-FOOT CLASSIC GAR WOOD RUNABOUT AND A 28-FOOT LEYARE.

flowers aboard. It's a tradition that the Andrew McNally continued throughout his ownership. The houseboat was moored in a quiet bay sheltered from the main shipping channel by Isle Royal at McNally's Wellesley Island property for 60 years. It was Andrew McNally's preferred summer residence until his recent death. The magnificent houseboat and its furnishings were bequeathed to the Antique Boat Museum in Clayton and will become a major attraction in their permanent collection.

THE 114-FOOT *LA DUCHESSE* IS ONE OF AMERICA'S GREATEST VINTAGE HOUSEBOATS. SUPERBLY MAINTAINED BY THE MCNALLY FAMILY, IT WILL SOON BE PERMANENTLY EXHIBITED AT THE ANTIQUE BOAT MUSEUM IN CLAYTON, NEW YORK.

AMARYLLIS

Around the turn of the century a great many large houseboats were used as summer residences in the Thousand Islands. Eighty-, ninety- and one-hundred-foot houseboats were seen frequently on the river during this period. Some houseboats served as quaint extensions of their owners' large summer homes, others were quite mobile and traveled to a variety of interesting locations, including the quiet lakes and bays along the Rideau Canal system.

Amaryllis is one of the great old houseboats of the Thousand Islands. It was designed and built in Cape Vincent, New York, in 1911 by Leon Peo for Commodore Gillespie as a comfortable summer residence. The Gillespies had a fine cottage on Basswood Island between Thousand Island Park and Clayton. Their 106-foot houseboat has a riveted steel hull that is 22 feet wide with a two-story wooden superstructure above the deck. On the main deck level is a large kitchen that connects to the dining room. The four guest staterooms have their own private bathrooms. Located on the grand upper level is a spacious living room with a fireplace that connects to the owner's stateroom and bath. Further aft are quarters for domestic staff and crew. *Amaryllis* has been in the same family for several decades and currently operates as a charming bed-and-breakfast near Rockport, Ontario.

THE 106-FOOT HOUSEBOAT *AMARYLLIS* WAS BUILT IN CAPE VINCENT IN 1911.
IT REMAINS PERMANENTLY MOORED IN THIS QUIET COVE AT CLUB ISLAND, WHERE IT OPERATES
AS A UNUSUAL BED-AND-BREAKFAST INN DURING THE SUMMER.

THE UPPER DECK ON THE HOUSEBOAT *AMARYLLIS* IS THE PERFECT PLACE
TO ENJOY RIVER VIEWS FROM THE COMFORT OF OLD WICKER.

BELORA BOATHOUSE

One of the finest vintage island boathouses in the Thousand Islands is located on Cherry Island and connected to the Belora residence. Prominently located at the foot of Cherry Island, Belora and Olympia were known as the Twin Cottages. These 50-room cottages were the summer homes of Manhattan department store partners Abraham & Straus. In the late 1930s both cottages were sold to a Syracuse businessman, and the property has remained in his family ever since. In the boathouse slips are the owner's superb 1940 26-foot Hutchinson lapstrake sport utility boat and their attractive 1937 Gar Wood runabout. Both boats have resided in this boathouse since they were purchased new over 60 years ago. Inside the frame building, at dock level, is a large workshop and storage racks for several St. Lawrence rowing skiffs, some of which date back to the turn of the century. The boathouse provides these vintage boats superb protection so that they remain in excellent condition and can be used regularly by their owners. The spacious second floor is a complete residence that once provided living accommodations for the domestic staff. In recent years, the boathouse has become a popular residence for younger members of Belora's family.

LOCATED ON THE QUIET SIDE OF CHERRY ISLAND, BELORA BOATHOUSE PROVIDES PLEASANT LIVING QUARTERS FOR DOMESTIC STAFF, SLIPS FOR THREE POWERBOATS, A WORKSHOP, INSIDE SKIFF STORAGE AND CONVENIENT GUEST DOCKAGE.

THE INA ISLAND BOATHOUSE

One of the largest of the great old boathouses of the St. Lawrence River is the enormous frame structure on Ina Island. With its many fine slips and hauling devices, it was home to a wide range of boats. However, the Ina boathouse may be best remembered for the wonderful dances and social events that were once conducted in its marvelous upper-level ballroom. The Ina Island boathouse ballroom was much larger than that of any local hotel. When dances were not scheduled, the ballroom became a full-size gymnasium. Several rooms on the upper floor were used as staff quarters.

INA ISLAND'S GRAND BOATHOUSE IS STILL STANDING AFTER 80 YEARS.
THE UPPER LEVEL OF THIS MAGNIFICENT BUILDING HAS SEVERAL GUEST
ROOMS ALONG ITS PERIMETER, AND A LARGE CENTER ROOM DOUBLES
AS BOTH GYMNASIUM AND BALLROOM.

THE CHALET BOAT PORT

Another variation in the style of boathouses is the boat-port type, in which the roof is simply supported by columns, leaving the sides completely open. The gently sloped roof provides all the necessary protection from the direct rays of the sun and the advantage of constant ventilation that is so important to the longevity of wooden boats.

THE RUSTIC BOAT PORT LOCATED BY THE SWISS CHALET ON WELLESLEY ISLAND
PROVIDES THE NECESSARY PROTECTION OF A ROOF WHILE PERMITTING THE FREE FLOW
OF FRESH AIR SO ESSENTIAL TO EXTENDING THE LIFE OF WOODEN BOATS.

PARTY WALL BOATHOUSES

This row of colorful boathouses share much in common. When the need for a boathouse exceeds the amount of shoreline available, a row of connecting covered slips may be the only practical solution. At Thousand Island Park the amount of available shoreline for individual boathouses was exceeded long ago by the number of boats owned by residents. The color of each boathouse helps identify which slip each boat owner occupies, as well as making for a very colorful shoreline.

THE SHARED-WALL BOATHOUSES OF THOUSAND ISLAND PARK ARE VIBRANT ENOUGH
TO CHEER UP ANY BOATER ON A GRAY DAY AND ADD A COLORFUL ACCENT ALONG
THE WATERFRONT OF THIS WELL-DECORATED COMMUNITY.

CROSSOVER ISLAND LIGHTHOUSE WAS BUILT IN 1848 AND IS LOCATED ONE MILE DOWNRIVER FROM CHIPPEWA POINT ON THE AMERICAN SHORE. AS ITS NAME INDICATES, IT WAS STRATEGICALLY BUILT AT THE SECTION OF THE RIVER WHERE SHIPS WOULD CROSS OVER FROM THE MAIN CHANNEL TO EITHER THE CANADIAN OR THE U.S. CHANNELS. IT WAS DECOMMISSIONED IN 1942 AND HAS BEEN PRIVATELY OWNED SINCE 1969.

LOCATED DIRECTLY ACROSS FROM BOLDT CASTLE, THE SUNKEN ROCK SHOAL WAS A TERRIBLE HAZARD TO NAVIGATION. THIS LIGHTHOUSE IS BUILT ON THE SHOAL AND HELPS GUIDE LARGE CARGO SHIPS AS THEY APPROACH THE AMERICAN NARROWS TRAVELING UPRIVER.

THE ROCK ISLAND LIGHTHOUSE MARKS THE NARROWEST AND MOST DANGEROUS POINT
ON THE ST. LAWRENCE SEAWAY'S SHIPPING CHANNEL, DIRECTLY ACROSS FROM THOUSAND ISLAND PARK.
THE FIRST LIGHTHOUSE WAS LOCATED HERE IN 1847. IT WAS REPLACED IN 1882 WITH THIS
40-FOOT TOWER. IT BECAME AN AUTOMATED SIGNAL IN 1941.

THE 69-FOOT TIBBETTS POINT LIGHTHOUSE WAS BUILT IN 1827. IT MARKS THE ENTRANCE TO THE ST. LAWRENCE RIVER ON THE AMERICAN SIDE FOR SHIPS HEADING DOWNRIVER. THE ORIGINAL LIGHTHOUSE WAS REPLACED IN 1854 WITH THE PRESENT FRESNEL LENS LIGHT, THE OLDEST ON THE RIVER.

Bibliography

Alexandria Bay Chamber of Commerce. *Where the Islands Are*. Watertown, NY, c.1925.

Bayne Company, James. *The Thousand Islands and the St. Lawrence River*. Grand Rapids, MI, c.1900.

Bayne Company, James. *Souvenir of the Thousand Islands*. Grand Rapids, MI, c.1915.

Browne, George W. *The St. Lawrence River*. Weathervane Books: New York, NY, 1950.

Cavalier, Julian. *American Castles*. A.S. Barnes Co., 1973.

Columbia Encyclopedia, 2nd Ed. Columbia University Press: New York, NY, 1950.

Combined Boat Tours. *The Fairy Land of America*. Watertown, NY.

Coughlin, Richard. *St. Lawrence River*. Santway Photo-Craft: Watertown, NY.

Fischer, George & Bouchard, Claude. *Sentinels in the Stream*. Boston Mills Press: Erin, ON, 2001.

Fryer, Mary Beacock. *Pictorial History of the Thousand Islands*. Besancourt Pub: Brockville, ON, 1982.

Godine, Amy. "The Ties That Bind," *Adirondack Life*, Sept-Oct. 2003.

Jury, Mark. "The Thousand Islands," *Look Magazine*, p.82-85. New York, NY, Aug. 1979.

Hanmer, Trudy J. *The St. Lawrence*. Franklin Watts: New York, NY, 1984.

Lastier, Margaret McCormick. *The Thousand Islands: Vacation Paradise*. Ogdensburg, NY, 1952.

Lesstrang, Jacques. *Seaway*. Superior Publishing: Vancouver, BC, 1976.

Lucas, Roger S. *Boldt's Boats*. Research Review Publications: Cheektowaga, NY, 1998.

Lucas, Roger S. "Boldt's First Visit," *The Thousand Islands Sun*. Alexandria Bay, NY, July 8, 1992.

Lucas, Roger S. "George C. Boldt," *Research Review*. Kenmore, NY, 1983.

Lynch, Don. *Titanic: An Illustrated History*. Madison Press: Toronto, 1992.

Malo, Paul. *Boldt Castle: In Search of the Lost Story*. The Laurentian Press: Fulton, NY, 2001.

Malo, Paul. *Fools' Paradise*. The Laurentian Press: Fulton, NY, 2003.

Malo, Paul. "The Thousand Islands," *New York Alive*. Albany, NY, July/Aug 1983.

Matthews, Robert. "Collectibles of the Thousand Islands," *The Gazette Annual*. Clayton, NY, 2003.

Northrup, Frank. "All Mourn George C. Boldt," *The Hotel Bulletin*, Jan. 1917.

Rielly, Jim. "Melancholy Mansion," *Syracuse Herald American*, Sept. 19, 1999.

Santway Photo-Craft Co. *Thousand Islands*. Watertown, NY.

Walsh, George J. *A Tour of the Thousand Islands*. Washington, DC.

Wiley, Day Allen. "A Thousand Island Estate," *Architectural Record*, Vol.25, p.125-130.

Acknowledgments

We wish to thank the homeowners and friends who helped make this book enjoyable to create. Summer homes seem always to hold a special place in the hearts of their owners. Opening one's own quiet and very personal summer retreat to be photographed for a publication can feel a little like hosting an invasion. We appreciate the kindness and sincere interest expressed by so many Thousand Islanders in helping make this project a reality. We are especially grateful to Philip Amsterdam, Karin and Pieter Bergen, Francis Crosby, Richard Lenhard, Teddy McNally, James O'Neill, Regina and Irving Rosen, Helena and Robert Skelding, Anne Thompson, Addison Vars, Ralph Watson and others who contributed stories and references. Paul Malo deserves my very special thanks for his contributions.

Anthony Mollica Jr.

A special thanks to Sue Halsey for her hospitality and making her home my home while I was photographing the region. For getting me around by boat, I would like to thank Ted Mowers and David Squires. For the amazing air boat rides in winter, my thanks to Gary Anderson and Wayne Green. For allowing me to visit the Singer Castle (off-season), I would like to thank Deborah Lack and Deborah Scholes. Finally, I would like to thank Gary DeYoung, Suzanne Bixby and everyone at the Thousand Islands International Tourism Council for their support.

George Fischer